Mirror, Mirror

To Deb,
Happy reading!

Published by Debut Books

Mirror, Mirror by A B Endacott

Mirror, Mirror

*How narrative and storytelling
shapes our lives*

A B Endacott

DEBUT BOOKS

Published by Debut Books
hello@debutbooks.com.au
debutbooks.com.au

First published 2020
Text © A B Endacott 2020
Design © Debut Books

The moral right of A B Endacott to be identified
as the author of this work has been asserted.

 A catalogue record for this
book is available from the
National Library of Australia

ISBN 9780648937500 (Print)
ISBN 9780648937562 (eBook)

Editorial by Amy Lovat
Design by Katherine Larsen
Typesetting by Blue Wren Books
Printed in Australia by McPherson's Printing Group

For picking the original kernel of this idea
out of the (metaphorical) rubbish, and
for the clearsighted vision that has brought
Debut Books to life, I dedicate this book to Kat.

This book contains references to death, sexual assault, the Stolen Generation, mental health and LGBTQIA+ rights.

Dear Reader,

I would like to acknowledge the land of the Wurundjeri people on which I live, work and play. Aboriginal and Torres Strait Islander peoples are the traditional owners and custodians of this land and I pay my respect to past, present and emerging elders. Sovereignty has never been ceded. It always was and always will be, Aboriginal land.

It is with great excitement and pride that I introduce you to the Mini Collection, a series of physically small books on really big topics. These books aim to broaden accessibility to the themes within their pages, and to connect readers with conversations we might be curious about, wish to know more about, but don't necessarily know how to engage with. It is my hope that these books will challenge the way the reader thinks, helping us to change the narrative we tell ourselves, and the ones we've been told by others.

The Minis are designed to welcome readers into a space where we feel safe to learn and grow. I encourage readers to listen and connect and work towards changing—or retelling—stories that lead us towards being better humans to one another. May these books challenge us to see the value in our differences, breaking down the stigma, shame and fear of the 'other'. Intentional change needs to be made if we are to enable a future that is inclusive, equal and kind. We must stand together and take action.

Let us encourage the normalising of changing our opinions when presented with new information and holding each other accountable for our actions. Let us acknowledge the ways in which our privilege enables biased practices that directly influence the oppression of another person. It is a daily practice of relearning how to be a better human to all, regardless of race, gender, sexuality, disability or religion. It is an ongoing decision to question and make changes to the systems we navigate every day.

It requires effort to open our hearts to challenging our privilege, our internal biases, and those of the people around us.

If you believe in love, justice and equality for all, then you understand that this work is non-negotiable. Let us listen to people's stories and their fears. Let us challenge the status quo and redefine what an inclusive future looks like, and let's work hard to make it happen.

I believe reading outside our own experiences helps to reduce the ignorance that breeds discrimination and encourages empathy and solidarity despite our differences. There is a very good reason why Debut Books came to life and that is because of the stories we tell and are told, and how they shape the way we walk through the world.

I met Alice through Instagram and we connected over our mutual love of reading. We had been moving in the same #bookstagram circles for a while and in February 2019 she sent me copies of her first two self-published books. I fell in love with Alice's storytelling and the characters she brought to life; her books are clever, thought provoking and heart-warming. I will never stop telling Alice what a wonderful storyteller she is.

When I was in the early stages of planning the Minis, Alice and I were chatting one day and she mentioned the disappointment at her PhD thesis proposal being declined. We talked about what she wanted to write, and I asked to read the proposal. From the very first paragraph I knew that this piece was meant for Debut Books. It has been an honour, privilege and joy to work with Alice and begin this publishing journey together.

Mirror, Mirror is an important discussion on the power of stories and the way they shape society. Regardless of who we are, we are all storytellers. We produce and consume curated content that is representative of parts of our lives, yet not the whole. In the context of social media, we often pick and choose what stories we share about ourselves.

It is also important to think about who else is telling your story, and how. When we look at the current discourse on race and gender (to name a couple), we see the way those with privilege and power speak to what they believe is 'truth', and how far this is from the lived realities and experiences of those people being spoken about. It is damaging and threatening the basic human rights of people all over the world, including here in Australia. It is important to be critical when considering who is telling what story and ensuring that we listen to the people within the communities being spoken about, and the truths they share.

I am proud to be launching the Debut Books publishing list with this book and I hope with all my heart that you enjoy reading it.

Always,
Katherine Larsen
Founder, Debut Books

Part One

Why do we tell stories?

I am a storyteller.

It has been an intrinsic part of me for longer than I can remember. Stories just make inherent sense to me. It's the way my brain is wired. When I look at the world, I see it through the lens of how I might use words to describe it, to convey what I see into the mind's eye of another person.

For me, there is a certain magic to writing. The way words will dance across my mind and then be made manifest upon the page (or screen) is a beautiful act. Without transgressing into the realm of the overly sappy, it makes me feel as though I'm taking a part of myself and transforming it into something that can reach beyond the limitations imposed by a single body and a single mind.

Before I was a storyteller myself, I was a consumer of stories. The first stories told to me were those of my parents as they taught me to talk, walk, understand the world and my place in it. They were storytellers, too, even if they didn't realise it.

That's the thing — we are all storytellers. We all navigate the world through narrative, through the tales we spin and which are spun for us.

Reading was not just something I learned to do. It was something I learned I could not live without. Like many, when I discovered the capacity for a book to pull me into a world that was wholly different from the one I inhabited, I voraciously consumed everything within reach. Books had — and still have — a way of absorbing me completely. Once I am in the world of the narrative, speaking with me becomes impossible; I simply *have* to know what happens.

Under my greedy eyes and impatient fingers, tomes tumbled.

When I think about my time in primary school in suburban Melbourne, Australia, in the late nineties, I remember heaving stacks of books to and from the library, and sitting on concrete steps outside a classroom at recess and lunchtime because I didn't want any more distraction from what I was reading than was necessary. It's not the whole portrait of my time at primary school, but it's the story that I tell most frequently about how I remember the formation of this vital aspect to my personhood.

This is not a unique experience. In any primary school class, there is a child who can barely be pried away from a book, but it's a story that's important to me and my understanding of who I am.

Books aren't the only kinds of stories to be told and heard. Stories are everywhere. In movies, in our TV shows, in artwork, in newspapers, and in the simple day-to-day information that we relay to one another.

We all tell stories, all the time.

It's not radical to claim stories are integral to how we communicate. If we want to be *very* technical, we could define story as a coherently organised series of information units that are conveyed through a medium whose meanings are pre-agreed upon by the recipient/s and the teller.

This means simply relaying a piece of information is a form of storytelling.

"Alex needs help lifting the milk" is a story, if a reasonably dry (pun only a little bit intended) one. The language is the pre-agreed upon method of communication, and we have our narrative elements: Alex, the protagonist, has embarked upon a quest, lifting the milk. But they have encountered an obstacle, its weight!

Obviously, it's more humdrum than an epic fantasy, but the point is that this remains the basic mechanism for how we convey information, regardless of whether it's for immediate practical use ("careful, the plate is very hot!"), or if it's a piece of fictionalised imagining.

Another way of defining story, I'll borrow from others. A sociologist named Clifford Geertz claimed culture is constituted by the stories we tell ourselves about ourselves; while philosopher and gender theorist Judith Butler posited in her

1988 essay *Performative Acts and Gender Constitution* that gender (to be distinct from biological sex) is defined by societal expectations, and that definition is reinforced by the act of 'performing', or 'telling the story' of that definition. But Butler's comment doesn't just apply to questions of gender identity. If you think about it, we tell ourselves a story about our identity ("I am the granddaughter of immigrants", "I will always have dessert"), which we tell other people. The act of telling that story gives people information about who we are and affirms for ourselves touchstone elements to our identity that drive not only our worldview, but our actions, too. Storytelling can therefore also be understood as a performance of identity. As a result, we could say that the concept of ourselves and our society is perpetually being constructed and reconstructed through stories (Ryan 525).

When we speak about ourselves or our families, or even our societies, I'd argue that fundamentally, we tell the version of the facts, elements, and story that we want to tell at that particular time. I have little interest in delving into a naval gazing discussion on the subjectivity of truth. Instead, I'll say that we frame things in certain ways, omit particular details, or emphasise others. And we do it about ourselves, too.

A really obvious example to point to is social media. We only need to glance at social media in order to see that everybody — and I do mean everybody — posts specific content that offers a limited and directed view of their lives, which leaves the viewer with a specific impression. It's taken to the extreme with influencers whose curation of their content conveys non-stop glamour (even with those behind-the-scenes shots, which supposedly draw back the curtain on certain 'perfect' pictures, the choice is a deliberate one and itself serves the construction of the narrative). Most of the time, this takes place on a subconscious level. People post what they like, or what they think looks good, or even simply what they feel comfortable posting. That may be content about food, or family, or travel, or pets. The curated content is a story; in this case, the one we want others to see and take as true about our lives and who we are. Social media is an example — a specific one to be sure — where it is possible to see an externalisation of something we do instinctively and intrinsically: we craft the story we want to tell about ourselves.

So what about books? How exactly does fiction fit in to this? At the most fundamental of levels, I believe the fiction we tell is a reflection of the author's perspective on the world around them.

If you'll indulge me, I'd like to illustrate this point with my own books.

My published books are all fantasy. They are set in a world wholly different to our own. And yet, they are directly inspired by things I see in the environment surrounding me.

Queendom of the Seven Lakes, a duology about an assassin who is hired to protect the first male heir to the throne, was inspired in part because I was sick of encountering the tired trope of the uproar over a woman ruling. To shine a light on just how ridiculous the perpetuation of that piece of narrative is, I flipped the genders. One of my favourite parts in the entire series is when one character cites aspects of 'male' behaviour and characteristics as evidence to why men are unsuitable to rule.

I took that a step further with *Ruthless Land*, which is set in a society where men are a subjugated group, to the point that they are forced to wear veils. It's important to note that the construction of the world was not intended to be a rebuke against the tradition of some Islamic cultures, which see women don some form of head covering. Instead, it's meant to look at how prejudice works, and how it is indoctrinated across an entire society.

The *Dark* trilogy was inspired by a thought I had one day when I was at university and Islamic State (IS) was at its apex (remember them? As I pen this during the Stage 4 Covid-19 lockdown in Melbourne, I feel a certain nostalgia for those days). We were looking at the way IS forced people in the territory it captured to behave in strict accordance with their (very narrow and self-serving) interpretation of the Qur'an. I wondered how I would react if a group of very unpleasant people rolled across my home, knocked on my door, and told me that if I didn't adhere to their decrees, I would be shot. Most of us like to think that we'd join the rebellion immediately, or refuse to bow down to the petty decrees of brutal tyrants. But I am quite attached to being alive, and to the safety of those I love. Thus, the Freya to whom we are introduced, was created.

In what I wrote, I created a mirror to what I saw. A book reviewer discussing my work (which is always wonderful for my ego!) summarised what I wish I'd articulated. Of the world I've built, she said:

> "It's a fantasy world, she's created a world, but she's created so much that contextually, from the world around us, that you understand it without having to think about it." (Mad Cheshire Rabbit)

I take inspiration directly from the surrounding world. I might flip it, or play with it, or do something unusual with it, but at the core, within the context of my fantasy writing, I play with things I see. Brandon Sanderson (an author I admire) says very specifically that while people often say fantasy writing draws on the past, he believes, in fact, it is fundamentally about the present (Flood). It's certainly true of my writing, and I think it's even true about science and speculative fiction; authors look at truths about the world today and consider how that will play out in ten, twenty, one hundred years. Books and stories — they're a mirror to who we are and where we are now.

I attended the Emerging Writers Festival in Melbourne a few years ago, and one of the festival patrons in the opening address said something to this effect: "Nobody is as maligned a group as writers are. Wherever you go, when you tell people that you're a writer, you will always hear the reply *oh yeah, I write, too*."

There are several truths behind that comment, but perhaps not all of them are what he intended to convey. While some of us are sufficiently deranged to stick at storytelling to transform the private act of putting down words into something for public consumption, that doesn't minimise the significance of the fact that so many people write. Be it for leisure, as an outlet, or even as an aspiration, the prevalence of people who write tells us about the power of stories — the ones we read, watch, hear, and tell ourselves.

And yet. People who write fiction, unless it is literary fiction, are deemed purveyors of escapism.

Sometimes I think it's a wonder that people who write fiction haven't been accused of drugging the masses. In the last year or so, I've become familiar with the theory of a literary anthropologist by the name of Wolfgang Iser. I'll refer back to him a few times, so get ready to hear a lot about our mate Wolfie. (In case you're wondering, anthropology — which I studied in my undergraduate degree — is the study of people; more specifically, of how groups and communities have specific identities, and how these identities are constructed and maintained by behaviours, ways of thinking, and norms. Literary anthropology looks at how communities are created and maintained by literary works.)

Iser wrote in one of his more seminal texts, *The Fictive and Imaginary*… well, he wrote a lot of things, and I'll be honest, it's a hard read. But one of the things I easily understood was the comment that the need to marginalise fiction speaks to its power

11

(Iser 112). Stories are powerful things. Books are powerful things. This is why people burn and ban them. To appropriate a quote from *V for Vendetta*, books and stories contain ideas, and ideas are bulletproof.

We write and tell stories not only to express ourselves, but to help understand a huge, often-scary, complex, multifaceted and multilayered world, of which even the most well-travelled of us only manage to see a tiny fragment. Stories give us the power to not only *see* a different world, but to inhabit it. This immersion has a power that is often referred to, but infrequently unpacked. Empathy — *true* empathy — is the ability to under-stand the experience and feelings of another. Put another way, it's the ability to put yourself in another person's shoes. Our friend Iser wrote a whole book discussing how and why the space of a text can do this. To save you the trouble of reading *The Fictive and Imaginary* (although I can't imagine why you'd possibly avoid ploughing through dense academic prose), I'll sum up the key points here:

- The 'world' of any story is crafted using elements of our own world so the reader can understand the narrative elements (the plot and its progression).
- Because this textual world is therefore like our world but not, it is a conceptually limbo space, where we suspend a lot of the mental processes that mean we accept or reject something out of hand, in keeping with our established views and norms.
- As a result, we are more likely to begin to entertain things that may challenge our preconceived notions, and open us up to new ideas and new ways of looking at the world.

This is powerful.

Sometimes text may simply be a 'space for play' — an opportunity for the reader to go somewhere (conceptually, of course) where they may otherwise not. Sometimes the story may be deeply transformative, leading the reader to quite literally slip into the shoes of a person for whose life they have almost no frame of reference and thus no other way to empathise. It's quite interesting to unpack how this actually functions, but I'm going to go into it a bit later.

In my writing, I try to blend those two ideas. Bearing in mind my relative privilege as a White woman living in a developed country with a strong democracy, much of my writing does fall along the lines of space for play.

My big passion as an educator, thinker, and human being, is critical thinking—asking people to consider the nuances of a situation, of people's motivations, of both sides of the story. It's why *The Quiet American* by Graeme Greene (1955) is such a great book—in Greene's own words, the characters inhabit worlds of grey. There is no clear 'good' or 'bad' person, no clear right or wrong answer; those binaries simply don't exist in the world of the story. Similarly, Hayao Miyazaki's films often explore this idea, too. It's perhaps most prominently brought to the fore in *Princess Mononoke* (1997), but across virtually all of his work, the villainous characters are rarely cartoonishly (ha!) evil, but imprisoned within the limitations of their worldview and their inability to move beyond this narrow set of thoughts and values.

Don't worry, I'm not comparing myself to Greene or Miyazaki. My ego has not yet reached that size. But I'd like to think that I at least do what I do well. I'm interested in the fact that the world is inhabited by people who are neither wholly good, nor wholly bad, they're just people. I think it's so vital to examine complexities of various situations. I try to explore that in my writing.

- In the *Dark* trilogy, the 'good guys' — the subjugated Pious — do some very questionable things in the name of rebellion. Similarly, the 'bad guys' — the dictatorial Kade — have brought reforms to the city that benefit many.
- In *Ruthless Land*, without giving away spoilers, people behave in objectively bad ways but for complex reasons that are the result of personal misfortune and the injustices of a society pushed upon them.
- In *Queendom*, Halen Katan comes the closest to the most out-and-out villain I've ever written,

but even he has valid points at times. More relevant, the series' starting point from Elen-ai's perspective is that the prospect of a man ruling the country is all kinds of wrong — it's a slap in the face to history, it's a move that will likely destabilise the country, and it's also stupid because men are poorly suited to rule. However, those axiomatic assumptions are challenged across the series, and we end with her having acknowledged her prejudices (if not failing to entirely overthrow them), and accepting where she was wrong.

Because of the perspective of the central character, obviously I ultimately prioritise their worldview, although I try, where possible, to at the very least confront my characters with the truth that what they believe may be true for them, but may not be *the* truth. The *Dark* trilogy certainly has action, but it also has a lot of reflection — a lot of the action takes place in Freya's head. If you like that sort of thing, you'd call it a very cerebral book. If you don't, you might call it boring. The reason for that, though, is because of the space for play—the critical thinking mindset in which we ask, 'How do I know that this is true?' is a key part of Freya's character development. In crafting the story, I hoped to emulate the 'shades of grey' aspect I love so much in *The Quiet American*—while Freya does ultimately make a decision, it's by no means necessarily the right one, and thus turns the question back to the reader to consider. I think a lot of really great stories do that.

Another academic who I really like, Roland Barthes, described narrative in one of the most beautiful ways I can possibly imagine. He described it like a fugue, pulling in new material while holding on to old material (255).

In music, a fugue has a short melody that is 'developed' across the piece—it might be played in different voices, transposed into a different key, or inverted. I like Barthes' analogy a lot because it makes sense to me; it's how I see stories: The exposition establishes the key information, and that's developed, inverted, played with, and generally explored as the story progresses. It could just as easily apply to how stories function as a mirror to society: they use the 'old' material of aspects of society, and then pull in new material on top of it to create and develop the story. I think it's beautiful.

Part Two

Why do we retell stories, and what does that say about them (and us)?

If you'll indulge me, I'd like to explore in a little more detail this idea about how exactly stories function as a sort of mirror. I'd like to do it by focusing on something of particular interest to me: the way we retell stories. And, by the way, strap yourself in, because in this section, I'm using footnotes.[1]

---

1 Yes, I know, they're the domain of the wanker, but especially when I get into really technical stuff,

From myth, to folklore, to history, we as humans seem to be fascinated by specific tales, weaving them anew again and again and again. I'd argue we refresh the tales because we want them to be enduring in their relevance. After all, a story is only listened to and passed on if people can relate to it in some way. Perhaps those specific stories we can't quite give up, even as time and technology distances us from their original format, because at their core, they are about some fundamental, intrinsic piece of human nature. Think of the myth of Orpheus and Eurydice, or of Psyche and Cupid[2]—the battle between blind faith

---

especially when it's arguably tangential to the broader point I'm trying to make, I'd prefer to give you all the option of not reading it, or coming to the material at your leisure rather than interrupting the flow of what I'm saying. Plus, I quite like how Jay Kristoff used them in the *Nevernight Chronicles*, so maybe they aren't all bad. I wouldn't be caught dead using them for citation, though.

2   In case you aren't familiar, they're respectively an Ancient Greek and an Ancient Roman myth; Orpheus and Eurydice is a little easier to compact: Orpheus' wife, the beautiful Eurydice, is tragically killed by snakebite on their wedding day. He descends into the underworld

and the desire to peek, to *know* — the temptation to confirm something for ourselves — is one that we encounter time and time again across the course of our lives. Think about it — how many times has someone said, "trust me", and you've gone and checked for yourself? However, I would need a far longer word count than here — and the resources of an entire institution at my disposal to test that hypothesis. What I'm instead going to do is look at how the varying retellings of one particular story tells us something about our society. To do that, I'm going to look at Cinderella, the Brothers Grimm, and Disney.

---

and begs Hades, lord of the dead, to allow him to take his wife back to the world of the living. Hades consents, but says Orpheus must lead his wife out and not look back. At the very edge of the border between life and death, Orpheus glances back, and Eurydice, who was behind him all along, is lost to him. There's some other stuff in there about him playing the lute, but for the purpose of my point, it's not strictly relevant. Sad stuff. But ask yourself this: would you have been able to walk all the way back without turning your head?

The happiest place on earth?

The Walt Disney Company was founded in the 1920s during the silent film era. It swiftly established itself as an early adopter of new technologies, for example, employing the first use of synchronised sound in *Steamboat Willie* (1928). However, it is arguable that the Disney empire only truly began in 1937 with the release of *Snow White and the Seven Dwarfs*, the first of its famous animated films in the format we know and love today. As Disney's popularity grew, so too did its reach and offering, from film to television, merchandise, and, of course, the creation of Disneyland. That the slogan of Disneyland is 'the happiest place on earth' attests to the place it sought and continues to seek in the hearts and minds of all who know of it.

The park's very design creates an immersive experience where visitors can 'meet' the beloved characters they have watched time and time again, while even 'travelling' through those fictitious worlds. This presumably cements the prominence of these narratives in the minds of all who visit the parks — and a great many of those who do not; I for one, have never been to Disneyland, but I certainly know all about it (and resented my parents for not taking me when I was younger). This alone is an interesting space for study — the creation of an immersive experience and the way it resonates with audiences has lessons for those in business and literature alike. It has been argued that the design and layout of the parks present a particular morality and way of life that is an idealised version of American society (Rojek). Indeed, the suggestion that Disney as a company is conveying a particular and specific message is not a new one, yet little work to unpack that claim or its implications has been done.

Disney is an interesting company. In any Anglophonic society, you'd be hard pressed to find someone who hasn't watched at least one of the Disney-brand films. However, with its acquisition across the last twenty years of various major cultural franchises (Pixar, Marvel, Lucasfilm, Twentieth Century Fox), in addition to its owner-ship of multiple distribution channels (Hulu, Buena Vista International, American Broadcasting

Company), it feels as though it would not be a stretch to say that one would be hard pressed to find many communities in the world who have not seen at least one piece of content that is not ultimately owned by Disney. To say this reach alone makes the company as a significant entity in the global landscape, would be a spectacular understatement. However, it's also worth noting how formative Disney is for so many. The animated Disney (and Pixar) films are some of the first people watch, often over and over again. There has been some study of the creation and cultural effect of Disney, but I'm not sure it looks holistically at the company as a conglomerate, nor at the way it reflects and affects the population who consume its content.[3] Disney has acquired various intellectual properties with

---

3 The most significant work on Disney's influence and position as a curator and producer of story seems to be a 2018 study conducted by de Leeuw & van de Laan, which established that young children watching Disney films are more likely to exhibit 'helping behaviour', as well as a 2020 update of a book titled *Understanding Disney: The Manufacture of Fantasy* by Janet Wasko.

specific cultural connotations; there is a discussion to be had about the possible homogenising effect of one single company controlling so many culturally significant producers of narrative.

Two things to consider arise here; first, how the various branches of the Disney corporation convey similar themes, messages and values, despite the nominal difference in the brands. Second, how a close reading of Disney films — especially the animated films and their remakes — may indicate a change in cultural demands and interest. To whatever extent Disney may push a certain message, their films must resonate with consumer demands, so how those stories have been changed, both in terms of content and presentation, says interesting things about the changes in the society watching those films.

Since its acquisition of the Marvel studio in 2009, some writing has been done on the Marvel franchise, most prominently collected in *Assembling the Marvel Cinematic Universe: Essays on the Social, Cultural, and Geopolitical Domains* (Chambliss et al). Yet the focus of study on the composition, messages, and cultural effect of the Marvel franchise does not extend to how the Marvel films may contain similar messages to that of the films under the original Disney branding. The fact alone that films under the Disney umbrella accounted for 38 percent of United States box office revenue in 2019 (The Economist) should merit examination of Disney narratives. Their cultural reach and influence is so significant that it seems irresponsible to not consider what messages Disney may be sending through its content.

In late February 2020, reports emerged that Disney had dropped the planned production of *Love, Victor*, a spin-off series to the 2018 LGBTQIA+ film *Love, Simon* as well as its plans to air the female-led remake of *High Fidelity*, owing to concerns that the subject matter was not "family friendly" (NBC News). Similarly, production on the reboot of Disney Channel original series *Lizzie McGuire* was suspended in early 2020, partly because of concerns that the content was too 'mature' for the family-friendly streaming service, Disney Plus, where it was slated to be launched. Series star Hilary Duff (and teen icon of my childhood) actually took to her

Instagram in late February to request that Disney executives consider moving the show to Hulu (the Disney-controlled streaming service has no ratings restrictions on its content). In a since-deleted post, she noted, "I'd be doing a disservice to everyone by limiting the realities of a 30 year old's journey to live under the ceiling of a PG rating" (Rosen).[4] While the censorship of certain content is hardly new, the scale of Disney's reach should at the very least merit some reflection on this behaviour and its implications. It is worth noting *High Fidelity* and *Love, Victor* did eventually go on air via Hulu. Disney's brand management strategy of siloing its various properties is an excellent one from a business perspective, but the reach of Disney and the way it so stringently controls the content of those various properties is nevertheless a subject for further investigation, given the significant number of people

---

4   As of the time of writing this piece, there has been no news as to whether Disney will give in to Duff's request, although she claims to be standing firm, and a strident fan campaign supporting her is ongoing (Viswanath). We can only live in hope.

who consume this content. As I said earlier, there is a significant lack of existing investigation (available to the general public, that is) into whether there is an underlying theme or agenda being promoted across these various brands. I don't have the space or knowledge to answer these questions here, but they are interesting, and worth reflecting on.

Disney is a fascinating company for three reasons.

First, it has sustained control over the creation and distribution of its content (continuing to this day with the existence of Disney Plus).

Second, the way in which Disney as a company is tied up with the identity of Walt Disney himself (Wasko). It's a lot easier to follow the story of a person — especially one who came from nothing and built a cultural monolith — than it is to conceptualise a corporation; think about how differently we view an airline as a company, compared to the way we view Disney. In part it's because of experiences; Disney creates products that generate positive experiences and memories, whereas even a single delayed flight can lead to a long-lasting negative association. It could also be because of the way the story of Disney himself has been crafted in popular imagining.

However, it's for the third reason that I'm writing about Disney now.

As a producer of narrative, Disney creates a totalising experience. Its first feature-length animated film, *Snow White and the Seven Dwarfs*, saw one of the first instances of tie-in merchandise and marketing campaigns. In the following years, Disney has broadened its offering to include television shows, Disneyland, Disney on Ice, and associated books. The stories it sells are lived out by the people who consume them in ways that are genuinely interesting. Moreover, Disney keeps its property relevant. Since 2015, we have seen the classic animated films being remade into live action films. A friend commented recently that it's a clever way of driving people back to rewatch the original versions, while also securing a new generation of watchers. It also strengthens the company's grip on the versions of the stories that it tells. In the relatively short space of words I have here (and also being keenly aware that not everybody is desperate to get into an extended discussion over questions of imagined spaces, fictive idealisation, or what code of narrative is being explored), I'm interested in what these remakes can tell us about our own society — what kind of mirror they may hold up not only about where we are, but how we've changed.

Cinderella, and the shape of stories

Time and time again, people like me who get really excited over the technical stuff discuss the fact that stories have a shape. More than that, they come back to the fact that stories have *similar* shapes: a lone hero fighting a monster to protect the community (*Captain America, James Bond*), encounters with a new world (*The Tempest, Avatar*), to name two of the most popular (Yorke).

Stories have to follow certain rules.

Why? Well, trying to answer that question in itself would require far more pages than this little volume contains, but if I had to be brief, I'd boil it down to the idea that the reader or audience (or whatever you want to call the person consuming the narrative) needs to be able to *enter* the world.

Our friend Iser seems to have a point here: the world of any story is a conceptual space we enter when we're watching or reading, or even listening to it.[5] There needs to be a 'doorway' of sorts that enables us to enter that half-created world. That doorway comes in the form of a story's predictable or familiar shape.

Why we need that predictability (although that feels too narrow a definition) is up for debate. The older I get, the grumpier I get, because I think the closest I will ever come to religion is adhering to structuralist theory.

Yes, yes, I know. I'm a big old nerd. In short,

---

5   I've not had a lot of time for the idea of audiobooks, but the recent audible version of Neil Gaiman's *Sandman* (first published in 1988) graphic novels seems to be doing interesting things in finding new ways to offer something that mere words on a page cannot. The same seems true for the audio versions of Jay Kristoff and Amie Kauffman's *Illuminae Files*, which feature a full cast of characters bringing to life a story told in effect across various mediums.

structuralism is a school of thought articulated by several theorists (Bronisław Malinowski, Émile Durkheim, Claude Lévi-Strauss, Vladimir Propp, Northrop Frye — a bunch of 'Old White Guys™' to be sure, but they said a lot of things that make a lot of sense… imagine how much *more* we'd know if women were involved in early fields of science, too!). It suggests that there is a universality across humankind; behaviours or customs that pop up across cultures which simply could not have interacted with one another for hundreds, if not thousands, of years, are taken as evidence of some fundamental constant in humans. Thus, societies we build will often have similar structures because of that innate… humanness.

When I first heard this idea, I thought it sort of made sense, but finding enough data to ever prove this particular theory to be true was impossible, so I was going to stick to functionalism[6] thank you very

---

6 Functionalism in this term is an anthropological theory developed by Bronisław Malinowski, Alfred Radcliffe Brown, and Marcel Mauss. It suggests that various cultural norms and behaviours serve a particular

much, and throw in a bit of exchange theory[7] for good measure. Yes, yes. Big. Nerd.

But the more I see of the world, the more I hear of the world, and the more stories and narratives from across the world that I see and read, the more I am forced to concede that there may be an underlying truth to some of what structuralist theory says.

This is quite a wordy preamble to explain why I'm personally so interested in retellings. I'm interested because we retell various story shapes all the time. Certainly, there are ongoing thematic threads, and similar 'shapes' (beginning, middle, end, anyone?) that consistently appear across the stories we tell.

---

function. That function often reinforces a particular cultural identity and provides a framework by which people are able to navigate the world around them in various ways; emotionally, socially, and practically. Ironically, Functionalism is often introduced in the context of 'structural functionalism'. Perhaps I should have known from the outset that I'd have to accept structuralism…

7   Marcell Mauss' work *The Gift* outlines the way in which relationships are premised upon mutual and equal exchange. I love it.

There are monsters to be slain, and sometimes to be understood (which is a different type of slaying), there are hearts to be broken, mended, and given away, and there are quests to be undertaken.

As I said, I'm particularly interested in how we actually retell the same story. The fascination this holds for me is because I think that in the various reinterpretations and retellings, we see how that story is a reflection of our own society, and they thus provide a vehicle for the storyteller to say something about where we're headed as well as where we currently sit.

Let's talk about *Cinderella*.

Fairy tales are a source of particular fascination to me for a variety of reasons, but perhaps it's because I, like almost every child who grew up in my English-speaking, largely Anglo-Saxon-based society, watched Disney films from a young age. Some of my earliest and warmest memories are of sitting on the couch with my grandfather as we watched *Robin Hood* for the umpteenth time. No matter how many times I wanted to watch it, he would always watch it with me. And it always made me feel safe. That memory takes on even more significance for me as I write this, because he passed away in June 2020, only a few weeks before I typed these words. That too, is a story, and one which can explain how other narratives, tales, and pieces of telling can become so powerful, so inculcated into our worldviews.

I had two versions of *Cinderella* on VHS (and if you don't know what that means, you are very young and I hate you).

One was the Disney version. I don't know who made the other version, but I liked it because one of the slippers wasn't shattered, so she still had a complete set. There were obviously other points of comparison across the films, but that's the one that has endured in my memory. Perhaps my interest in the retellings and various versions of fairy tales (and myths, and legends) can be traced to this. Perhaps not. Regardless, I was also made aware from a relatively young age that the versions of the stories I'd seen which offered swelling soundtracks and happy endings, were not the only — or indeed the original — versions.

I had a book of Hans Christian Andersen's stories
— perhaps with some of the more graphic wording
cut out, but the events were largely the same; in
Andersen's 1837 version of *The Little Mermaid*, the
titular mermaid's sisters cut off their hair so she can
return to the sea, provided she kills the Prince who
has married another woman, but she is unable to
bring herself to commit the act, so she allows herself
to turn to sea foam instead. Cheerful, I know. But the
original versions of many fairy tales were brutal and
more often than not didn't end happily. Why those
stories changed is an interesting question, and one
not often answered. More interesting to me, is what
those changes say about the changes in the society
to which the new version is presented. This is also a
question with not many answers.

So, to *Cinderella*.

I'm going to take us through the *Cinderella* retellings by primarily examining the French Charles
Perrault version — *Cendrillon*, the German Brothers
Grimm version — *Aschenputtel*, and the two Disney
cinematic versions (1950 animated and 2016 live
action remake). However, to my point about the

way in which we repeat stories, the Cinderella story is everywhere across culture and time. There is *Ye Xian* from China, which predates the Qin and Han Dynasty, *Rhodopis* from Ancient Egypt, or *Tăm Cám* from Vietnam.

While there are notable differences in the plot of all versions, there are recurring elements of the story that make it recognisable as specifically a Cinderella story: a young girl of kind and sweet disposition, left to the mercy of a cruel stepmother and step (or half) sister(s), a guardian or guiding figure who bestows upon her beautiful clothes, her appearing to a love interest of much higher status than her, a lost shoe, rediscovery, and elevation of social status through marriage.

Roland Barthes[8] said stories are transposable; they can be retold in a different setting while

---

8   You might remember our friend Iser. Iser claims to be a Literary Anthropologist, who drew on the work of Barthes. Barthes was one of the thinkers who contributed to the creation of an academic field called narratology, which combines literature, linguistics, and sociology. While his writing is really difficult to wade through, it's very thought provoking.

retaining their 'core'. Not all of those elements have to be present, but a significant number of them do in order for it to be a retelling. In addition, the story must follow a certain shape. There is a video of Kurt Vonnegut describing the shape of stories, paying particular interest to the Cinderella story. He notes that the shape of the Cinderella story is one that we as a culture find particularly appealing: At the story's beginning, the protagonist's emotional state is a place of relative sadness. A change in circumstances arrives, significantly elevating their happiness. Then, catastrophe! Something returns the protagonist to their original circumstances and they are even sadder than they were at the story's beginning. Then, one final shift arrives to restore the new state, and they end the story at the happiest they have ever been.

Certainly, the particular 'shape' can be seen not simply in rom-coms, but in various genres. Even superhero films often follow this story shape. Consider the 2019 DC film *Shazam* (it's a great film and if you haven't watched it, I recommend you skip the next few sentences): Billy is at a low point as his search for his birth mother has hit a dead-end. He is placed into a great new foster home with kind people, and then he gains superpowers. He and Freddy (his foster brother) have a great time as they explore the extent of his powers — riding high! Then Mark Strong comes in and beats Billy up (he realises he's not invincible but, in fact, is in danger). Freddy, fairly, lambasts Billy for wasting his powers, and Billy finds his birth mother and learns that she doesn't really want anything to do with him — lowest point. However, he realises that there are people who do want him, and this gives him the strength to defeat Mark Strong — riding high! Does that track like something else we know?

Once you see it, you kind of can't un-see it. I particularly look out for it in films. And I obnoxiously comment on it, too.

Off the top of my head, popular stories that have been *specifically* inspired by Cinderella include *Pretty Woman*, *50 Shades of Grey*, *Crazy Rich Asians*, *Throne of Glass*, and *Sex and the City: the Movie*. In addition to the popular narratives in which the key points of the story are taken and re-imagined, there's also the out-and-out retellings: *Ever After* and *A Cinderella Story* are two of the biggest films within popular culture from the last thirty years, but there are so many more. And that's not even going into the shape of the Cinderella story, which dominates almost every rom-com, and quite a few other genres of story.

But getting back to the matter at hand: Cinderella. It's an unusual experience to be living through the Disney remakes as they are being filmed and released. Having watched some of the films in question at or around the time of their release (the ones that came out in the 90s… I'm not *that* old) and then watching the live action remakes as they are released, it is interesting to see not only what has been changed in the tellings, but also in how I and the culture that receives the films, has changed.

Disney is a company that knows the value of telling a narrative to keep it relevant and important to the market it serves (the personal story of Walt Disney himself, remember?). It means that the films they make, in an environment that increasingly prioritises and advocates LGBTQIA+ rights, racial equality, and social justice more broadly, has to incorporate those elements into its new (or updated) offerings. While some have criticised the company for being very slow in incorporating such elements into its stories, and when it has, for not doing enough, it remains significant that a company so enmeshed within the wholesome, very conservative American cultural identity is making changes such as the inclusion of aromantic storylines, more 'realistic' female body types, more racially diverse stories, and same-sex relationships.[9] Remember, the company has a significant interest in not losing customers, so anything too radical, and it will lose a large swathe of its domestic customer base (this is, after all, the country that regularly elects hyperconservative individuals to office).

---

9 *Moana* (2016) has no romance, she is Polynesian, and her form was specifically designed to be not stick-thin, while *Frozen* (2013) has a scene that features the owner of 'Wandering Oaken's Trading Post and Sauna' alongside his husband and children — it's not putting the relationship front-and-centre, in fact, it's arguably blink-and-you'll-miss-it, but its inclusion is a huge step for a company that has a history of being so very conservative.

First and foremost, Disney is a company, so the need to stay relevant as a creator of narrative is key to its capacity to remain profitable. Yet the way the content changes, especially when we can compare the different versions side by side, tells us something interesting about how our society has changed.

The Brothers Grimm and their Disney-fication

I think there's a very obvious parallel to be drawn between the Brothers Grimm and Disney films. Not simply because both are curators of fairy tales (more or less), but because the Brothers Grimm also retold their stories over the years.

Jacob and Wilhelm Grimm produced their first collection of fairy tales, *Children's Stories and Household Tales*, in 1812. The work itself was part of the German nation-building project, set against the backdrop of the Napoleonic Wars, and undertaken initially as a scholarly exercise to record folk tales as evidence of a German national identity and shared cultural history rather than to service mass consumption. Yet the *Tales* proved unexpectedly popular, and so the brothers re-wrote the stories seven times across nearly five decades to make them more accessible to a market populated by the average citizen (Dégh 88). Professor Jack Zipes notes the various editions of their collections became increasingly "aesthetically pleasing literary works", which saw the inclusion of "Christian references, folk proverbs, ornate description, and moralistic comments" (20). For instance, the brothers removed overt references to premarital sex or pregnancy following readers' complaints, but left in graphic details of violence (Tatar xlix). They also removed stories from the *Tales* that were considered to have content inappropriate for younger readers, not fit with the theme of the rest of the tales, or be not German enough in origin. For example, *Hans Dumm* tells the story of a hunchbacked man whose wishes — including wishing that a beautiful princess becomes pregnant — come true. The allusion to premarital sex, in combination with the fact that a version of the story had appeared in an Italian fairy tale collection (Tatar 408), and possibly even the fact that the princess ends up being the voice of reason (what, a woman!?), would have contravened the patriarchal, conservative, *German* culture that the Grimms were trying to reinforce by collecting and publishing these stories.

The various iterations of the Grimms' stories provide rich fodder for exploration in to how culture shapes the telling of the story, not only in the stories' translation from academic to recreational text, but also in the way that the stories' content and ancillary material (i.e. the 'telling') shapes that culture. As noted, the brothers often left in quite visceral descriptions of violence. It is interesting to note that this violence was most often visited against immoral or villainous characters in some form of retribution (Tatar 1).[10] The act of deletion when it came to content relating to sex tells us something about

---

10 It is worth nothing that violence was, at times, censored. The tale *How Children Played Butcher With Each Other* (published only in the first version of the *Tales*), sees children visit against one another but without any clear framework of retributive morality through which to justify the brutality as we otherwise see in fairy tales.

the sensibilities of the culture in which the stories were published; one could easily speculate that violence was normalised by several aspects of the early nineteenth century, not least of which could be the Napoleonic Wars, which were such a threat to the nascent (and thus fragile) sense of German identity. It is therefore possible that violence was an expected part of the everyday, and thus perhaps it felt important to normalise violence for children.

The retellings of the Grimms' fairy tales offer a unique insight into how culture shapes narrative, as they crafted their versions to best appeal to the desires and interests of their readership. That readership, of course, changed over time and will continue to do so. The act of their revisions is a testament to that, as is the fact that the stories were taken and retold in different formats with changes to parts of the story.

The foundation of the Disney empire is retellings of fairy tales, many of which originated in Europe and contained darker, more gruesome elements than the 'happy ending' musicals of those first films. It might be easy to attribute these changes to the desires of a post-war American audience; however, that's a rather reductionist analysis of the cultural factors that may have influenced the narrative's production, and second, this lacks a certain depth of analysis by not examining what elements of the original narrative were left intact.

The fact that children across the globe watch Disney films repeatedly makes them even more susceptible to the messages within. The Branagh version's screenwriter, Chris Weitz, articulated this when he said of Disney, "I think they've got a tremendous sense of their sort of responsibility to the children of the world, because this is one company where you'd say that we were affected by them as children and as we become parents, we know that our children are equally going to be affected by what Disney makes" (Lussier).

The two most well-known versions of the European Cinderella fairy tales are the French *Cendrillon* (Perrault) and the German *Aschenputtel* (Grimm). Their story shapes are virtually identical, although there are significant differences between the details across the two:

- Cendrillon has a fairy godmother who gives her a glow-up; Aschenputtel is bestowed beautiful clothes by a white bird, and a magical hazel tree planted on her mother's grave; the birds also help her complete tasks set by her stepmother.
- Cendrillon's ball takes place over one night; Aschenputtel's takes place over three.
- Cendrillon is given glass slippers; Aschenputtel has golden embroidered slippers.
- Cendrillon has one sympathetic stepsister and one unkind stepsister, whereas both of Aschenputtel's stepsisters are horrible.
- Aschenputtel's stepsisters actually mutilate their feet to make the slipper fit; chirping birds draw the Prince's attention to the tell-tale blood.
- Cendrillon allows her stepsisters to come to court and even creates favourable marriages for them, while the birds peck out the eyes of Aschenputtel's stepsisters.

While the 1950 Disney version of *Cinderella* gives credit to Perrault's *Cendrillon* as its source of inspiration, and indeed the inclusion of the now-iconic

47

fairy godmother and glass slippers are taken directly from *Cendrillon*, one important aspect from the Grimms' telling of the story is imported: Cinderella's relationship with the natural world. The anthropomorphic animals who assist Cinderella in a variety of ways would seem to be directly inspired by Aschenputtel's close relationship to the birds living near her. The 2015 Branagh version would appear to include more elements from the Grimms' story. It clearly establishes Ella's (who is given a name rather than the title of Cinderella, leaving her original name obscured by that given to her by her abusers) connection with her parents and her devotion to her mother's memory, as well as her connection to the natural world; things emphasised by the Grimms.

Branagh's *Cinderella* also seems to find a compromise between the two tales; while the stepsisters of the 1950 *Cinderella* fall out of the story as soon as the glass slipper fits, Ella explicitly forgives her stepmother and stepsisters, although the narrator tells us that they leave the country and are never heard from again. While it isn't the literally bloody ending for the stepsisters that sees them mutilate their feet in desperate attempts to make the slipper fit, and have their eyes subsequently pecked out by the birds loyal to Aschenputtel, it is definitely not Cendrillon finding her stepsisters a place at court and making socially advantageous marriages for them.

These differences could be attributed to the decision of the director and writers, and the desire to pay homage to the source material of the original *Cinderella* tale. However, the fact that those decisions were made in the context of a mammoth company catering to mass demand to appeal to broader society, speaks volumes about the tastes and norms of that society — our society. A comparison between the two versions of the film can therefore reveal the differences — and similarities — in cultural norms across the sixty-five intervening years.

Arguably, the most striking difference between the two *Cinderella* films is in what transpires between her and the Prince. This can only be attributed to the change in gender roles and relations in the intervening several decades, and shows the way the stories we tell mirror society, but also how stories confirm aspects to our societal narrative and norms. Not only is the Prince given a name in Branagh's version — Kit — but he is given more than the seven or so lines that he utters in the 1950s version. In fact, we are privy to exchanges between the two protagonists that at least implies an intellectual connection, and shows Cinderella's capacity to be a good counterbalance to Kit who is a self-professed 'apprentice' in the 'trade' of ruling. The importance placed upon Ella's intelligence and strength being recognised, respected, and valued by Kit (which also marks perhaps the first iteration of the story that endows him with a name beyond that of his title, as indeed the film does for her, too), thus gives her a power that exists at a structural level, which is otherwise absent in the 1950 animated version, the Brothers Grimm versions, and Perrault's version.

Interestingly, *Aschenputtel* does state that the Prince and Cinderella spend three nights dancing and interacting, although the brevity of the story precludes the reader from knowing any part of these conversations. This stands as a contrast against *Cendrillon*, in which Cinderella's primary value lies in her physical beauty and fair heart. The Perrault characterisation would seem to be the version from which the 1950 film takes its cues, and from which the Branagh production deviates. This can be supported by observations of cultural norms since the 1950s that have come to laud and actively promote 'strong' women. In fact, the comments made by screenwriter Chris Weitz makes clear the change in cultural norms and the desire to play to these changes. Weitz noted that "the view of romance in the animated film is not particularly contemporary […] in terms of why she loves him or why she wants to go to him. I think these days, we demand more than that" (Brandon, 2015).

As I've previously noted, Disney obviously has to ensure the films appeal to their audience. The public increasingly has little appetite for a story featuring a passive female protagonist. However, the requirement of the story to be updated in order to appeal to a broad audience is interesting in itself. It would appear to confirm my belief that we want stories to act as a mirror, and how much stock we place in that mirror — we want to see ourselves affirmed, we look to stories to give us a perspective and picture that moves beyond the narrow confines of our subjective experience. In seeing these features of our society reflected back at us, we thus confirm them.

Yes, we believe women have a value beyond being attractive. *Yes*, we think that a good relationship is one in which the people actually share an intellectual connection and communicate with each other. *Yes*, we want people in positions of power to actually possess some humility about the limits of their capacity to lead.

Despite the heavy influence of the Perrault version in the animated film, elements from the Brothers Grimm version can nevertheless be seen across both versions. The 'fairy godmother' of Jacob and Wilhelm's Cinderella comes in the form of nature. *Aschenputtel* places an emphasis on Cinderella's relationship to her mother, her dedication to her mother's memory, and her consequent kindness. This kindness is rewarded as she goes to the magical hazel tree to request a proper outfit for the ball (the birds also warn of the stepsisters' deception in mutilating their feet to make the slipper—gold rather than glass—fit).

Iser examined the significance of the natural world in literature, noting that it was an idealised space in text that allows the reader to consider and view the story in a particular manner (58). In *The Fictive and the Imaginary*, he discusses the setting of a natural environment rather than the inclusion of natural elements; the point nevertheless remains about the power of the natural world in allowing readers to consider underlying messages within the narrative—messages they may not initially be willing to entertain. Iser can thus be understood to say that this relationship to the natural world and its rewards draws attention to the moral value of the time.

This could be seen to be reflected in Aschenputtel's filial devotion carried out through her nurturing of the hazel tree. One could suggest that the inclusion of the animals who assist Cinderella in the animated film is thus symbolic of her good nature. The point of contrast across the films here is that the audience knows virtually nothing of the parents of the 1950 film's Cinderella, or her relationship to them, whereas Branagh's version spends time establishing the importance of Cinderella's mother in shaping the person she becomes and her retention of the values of 'have courage and be kind'. Branagh's Cinderella also has assistance from animals, and although they neither talk nor sing, they perform the function of making the royal retinue aware of Cinderella's presence in the house, thus uniting her with the Prince.

In literature, a character's association with nature is often taken to be indicative of inherent moral goodness on the part of that character (Iser). The fact that the telling retains these aspects shows an interesting understanding of the natural environment and its connotations that remain despite the mass urbanisation that characterises modern living. Work has been done that suggests even during eras when humanity lived in environments far closer to the natural world, literary representations of nature were highly idealised (Iser). It stands to reason that any depiction of a natural world in any form of contemporary narrative is also highly idealised, rather than a perfect representation of the natural environment. However, it is difficult to find any work that examines how these idealised depictions may have changed, and what they may reflect about popular understandings of nature and the natural world.

In both films, Cinderella and Ella have a strong connection to nature — Cinderella can actually talk with animals (!) while Ella spends a significant amount of time in the fields. It's one of the key ways that we know both characters are good and kind people, and thus not deserving of the treatment they receive at the hands of their stepmother and stepsisters. More than that, it's a quick signifier to the audience that they'll make a good Queen. It's interesting that after all this time, we still view nature as 'pure' and 'good' (unless it goes in the completely opposite direction and becomes a place that harbours primordial evil — itself an interesting concept to unpack because there's an arguable aspect to purging of the corruption of humanity; Stephen King would be fertile ground to explore here) and the framing of a character with relation to nature is symbolic shorthand for their 'goodness'. But while it says something about how our society understands nature, it doesn't go towards explaining why we have such a specific view of it. Perhaps because in an increasingly urbanised, teched-up world, we idealise rural settings and unbounded meadows as a connection to the 'true' self, and to a simpler pace of life. Perhaps it's because of increased discussion around environmentalism putting nature as something important to us, and therefore, any character who exists alongside nature appears moral to us because they aren't plundering it for their own personal profit. Perhaps there's some psychological effect created by the colour green. Whatever it is, I can't claim to have any specific answers, but it's certainly food for thought, and shows that while much of our lifestyles and technologies have changed since the 1950s, certain deep-rooted (ha, what a pun!) understandings of nature and its importance haven't gone away.

Obviously, I've only provided one very specific example in this discussion: that of Cinderella.

There is often significant criticism for the proclivity of mainstream film studios to shy away from originality. True, it's a safer financial bet to use existing, proven intellectual property. But if the average consumer truly had no appetite for such repetition, studios would stop producing it. We keep telling, reading, and watching the same stories, and have throughout history.

Some claim that we re-watch familiar TV shows and movies, or re-read familiar books especially when they're going through a period of anxiety because there's a comfort in knowing how the story will unfold (Rocha). If the amount of *Frasier* I've watched across the Coronavirus pandemic is anything to go by, it's certainly true. However, the retelling of various fairy tales may speak to something deeper than that. At the very least, companies like Disney give nerds like me some really good data to be able to perform a clear side-by-side analysis. In so doing, the way stories specifically engage with parts of our society and culture is particularly obvious.

It's just a shame that Disney hasn't remade *Snow White and the Seven Dwarfs* yet, because there was such a great pun about mirrors that I could have used.

Part Three

Can stories change us for the better?

Stories have certainly changed the way I see the world.

When writing this, I initially penned that it is impossible for a story to not in some way challenge, or at the very least broaden, our worldview. Then I deleted it, because that's not entirely true.

There is a very small subset of people who exclusively consume narratives that only reinforce their existent worldview, from something as intimate as familial dynamics, to something as broad as politics. The way search engine algorithms work, which span across social media, too, ensures that we are constantly being presented with what we have established from previous behaviour as things we like (and believe). It means that to find things that might fall outside our regular zone of reading, watching, or even thinking, we need to actively look for them. When you take that and combine it with the innate inertia within human nature, you get people who don't really move beyond a certain scope.

I struggle with knowing exactly how to feel about this. On a purely principled level, it leaves me uncomfortable.

Ossification of thought is truly antithetical to me —without seeking out new information, new ideas, new *things*, I believe we cannot grow. However, principle is one of those things I'd argue should be like a guiding beacon, rather than a path etched in stone. I have to acknowledge that the hint about the purpose of leisure time is in the name. Should people be obliged to do something with which they're fundamentally uncomfortable and which is an act of intellectual labour to complete, especially when this is an activity nominally undertaken within the context of leisure space? Provided the TV shows and movies they're watching, or the books they're reading, aren't actively disseminating prejudice, should this be an issue?

I don't know.

I do know that I've read many 'traditional' narratives that have subtly introduced food for thought, or have worked hard to break down certain stereotypes without being overtly preachy. I think that's really important work, because things that are mass consumed are popular precisely because they're easy to read or watch, not because they offer an insightful critique about the role of gender or power structures across global communities.

At this point, I could easily diverge into a very long tangent about the question this raises about the obligations of authors and the debate therein. (In short, there is a school of thought that claims it is the responsibility of authors to 'better' society through the content of their work, precisely because stories have the power to change attitudes. While I broadly would say that yes, authors should be aware of this, the biggest problem I have with the stance is that it assumes authors exist in a groupthink and thus have exactly the same set of views on everything — a lot of authors are socially conservative and by that logic they too should be trying to push what they think is 'right', almost didactically, into their work. It also creates a dangerous attitude of moral superiority that I believe has the power to alienate audiences).

However, that's not what this piece of writing is about. This is about the how. *How* do stories change us? I'm going to explain by telling you a story.

I think it's been pretty clearly established by now that I'm a voracious reader. Without intending to sound too narcissistic, I think (or hope) I've also established that I'm reasonably well-informed, too. I know a lot of things, about a lot of stuff. It makes me quite the asset on a trivia team.

That means when I encounter people who make claims that I'll politely call interesting, I often have information at my disposal to be able to swiftly craft a (polite) counterargument. I'll offer an example.

When people talk about African American incarceration and crime rates, they may say something like "well the reason why black people are locked up at a higher rate is because they commit more crimes". That may be true. However, it also fails to look at *why* that may be true. Discrimination, disadvantage, and intergenerational poverty are significant contributing factors to crime rates.

The fact that there are still people alive who knew slaves (admittedly these people are *very* old), speaks to the proximity of an entrenched and codified discrimination in our cultural consciousness.

The fact that there are a lot of people who can still remember segregation — a number that grows if we consider the Apartheid regime — only serves to reinforce that.

I can speak to the longstanding effect of these structures, of the difficulty of dismantling that kind of institutionalised discrimination, especially when it is still practiced by so many people.

But for a really, really long time, I couldn't quite wrap my head around even a small fraction of what it must be like to be on the receiving end of those attitudes, norms, and even laws, which reinforce to a person at every possible stage of their life that they are considered lesser — deserve less — on the sole justification of skin colour. It was a book that gave me emotional knowledge, rather than simply intellectual knowledge.

You might have heard of *The Bluest Eye* (1970) by Toni Morrison. It's mentioned on the TV adaptation of *The Chilling Adventures of Sabrina* (2018–2020), and good on the show's writers for repping it!

I first read Morrison when I was in my penultimate year of school.

We studied *Beloved* (1987), which was inspired by the life of Margaret Garner, an African American woman who escaped her enslavement by crossing into a free state. When she was pursued, she killed her child rather than have her daughter taken back into slavery. The book is undeniably powerful, but I was more fascinated by the moral conundrum posed by the narrative, rather than the story it was telling about race.

Maybe I was too young. Maybe this was my first encounter with a narrative about race of this complexity. Regardless, it's a good book, and I recommend it.

I came back to Morrison only two years ago, when *The Bluest Eye* was on the syllabus (I tutor English and Literature for senior high school students). The central act of the novel is the rape of a young African American girl by her father. The story is about how such an act could be committed, and how, in Morrison's own words:

> "I focused therefore on how something as grotesque as the demonisation of an entire race could take root in the most delicate member of society: a child; the most vulnerable member: a female. In trying to dramatise the devastation that even casual racial contempt can cause, I chose a unique situation, not a representative one." (anniversary edition)

Morrison's polyphonic (multi-voiced) narrative takes the reader through the perspectives of many Bla(c)k characters across various stages of their lives and shows how the experience of being continually denied access, justice, and dignity on the basis of race leads to an internalised sense of diminished self-worth. Moreover, she deftly depicts the difficulty of caring for and nurturing your own child when you believe that you and anything connected to you is worthless.

I'm not doing the story justice, so if there is one book you are compelled to pick up from reading this, I recommend it be *The Bluest Eye*. The point is that it was only in reading this book that I began to understand the perniciousness of racism, and the way not simply rules and laws, but also looks, gestures, and comments, layer onto someone who is the subject of that prejudice, and how even the most resilient of people will find some of that seeping into their understanding of themselves, and their place within the world.

Similarly, it was only when I read *The White Girl* by Tony Birch that I understood the humiliations forced upon Indigenous Australians by the (ironically named) Protectorate system. The Protectorate Act claimed Indigenous Australian people were Australian fauna and thus denoted that they were confined to 'reserves'. Moreover, they were utterly subject to the whims of the Protector. They could not leave the area without permission, their lives were regulated up to and including education, marriage, and conduct. Any money they earned was given to the Protector to then pass on to them. Frequently, of course, it did not reach its intended end point. Tom Wright's play *Black Diggers* touches on this as one of the reasons why some Indigenous Australian men enlisted to fight in World War I, despite not even being considered citizens — and in fact being told that they are "physically deficient. Reason: Strongly Aboriginal in type" (Wright). Of course, that's without even touching on the regulations that came into force about 'half caste' Indigenous Australians, which became part of the legal infrastructure permitting the Stolen Generation.[11]

---

11 Each state had slightly different systems in place, but the series of legislation passed can be accessed, and is damning to read, especially when you read them one after the other. You can find them in the digitised collections on the Australian Institute of Aboriginal and Torres Strait Islander Stories (AIATSIS) website.

It was Birch's story about a grandmother whose love for her granddaughter is so great that she will risk everything in order to save her from being taken away under the Stolen Generation scheme, that made me really begin to start to understand what the experience might have been like. In *The White Girl*, the terror inspired by people who are meant to protect and uphold justice imbues every page.

Birch's story is one about love — it is inspiring and beautiful and well-written, so the darkness against which it is set is not the dominant theme. But it is inescapable. And while Birch notes that the events in the story are fictionalised imaginings based off real events, it is true that this was the lived reality for so many people, who "suffered the theft of their own blood" (Birch 263) and the resultant trauma of knowing that those loved ones had been taken away on the basis of nothing more than a racist system, and they were powerless to do anything about it. Odette, Birch's protagonist, refuses to be powerless. But the very real limitations of her agency are inescapable. It was only through reading this story that I began to even grasp at the understanding of the utter despair that being subjugated by such a system would invariably inspire.

I'd like to pause here and acknowledge that these are two specific examples providing microcosmic insights into the varying experiences endured by African Americans and Indigenous Australians. To claim that by knowing some things and reading a couple of books gives me any authority to speak on such matters would be the height of hubris. However, what it has done is impart upon me the obligations upon White society, to not simply provide 'equal opportunity' for people who have been historically marginalised and the subject of institutionalised disenfranchisement and discrimination, but to ensure that communities whose disadvantage today is the direct result of that historical discrimination are raised up. How? That's a little more difficult to answer.

The point is, stories offer insight that compels reflection and reconceptualisation; the stories offer a reflection to something we might not necessarily otherwise see. Let me give you an entirely different example.

Mental health is a term we employ with some frequency. As a society, we've come a really long way in recognising the importance of caring not only about our physical ailments, but our mental ones as well. Depression is a pervasive, sneaky illness — for some it's chronic, for some it's not necessarily a lifelong companion. But it has the capacity to wreak a destructive ruin on lives.

Strenuous awareness-raising work has assisted in broadening people's understanding of this condition as being more than simply 'sad feelings'. In Australia, government support alongside the fabulous work of organisations such as *Lifeline, Beyond Blue*, the *Black Dog Institute* and *Orygen Youth Health* (to name but a few), has done much to peel away the stigma associated with having depression, or seeking help for it.

And this is explored and reflected in books. The eponymous Lirael from book two of the *Old Kingdom Trilogy* by Garth Nix was a relatively ground-breaking figure when it comes to narrative depictions of depression. When we meet her, she is genuinely depressed — it's something that she struggles with over the course of her narrative arc. However, what I really appreciated within the world was that when she reappears in *Goldenhand*, her depression didn't disappear simply because of a change in circumstances. It's an honest and unflinching depiction of this mental illness that assists people in understanding what it is like to live with something that so profoundly affects one's experience of the world. Obviously, there are rays of light, but the nuanced depiction is one that enhances understanding and forges empathy, and this is what works in concert with other actors to actually facilitate a shift in attitude.

However, mental illness exists beyond anxiety and depression, which touches almost every life at some point to some degree (this claim is truer than ever, given the Covid-19 phenomenon and the effect of the Stage 4 restrictions on the mental health of the populace).

Mental illnesses have a complexity to them that is profoundly nuanced. Wai Chim's spectacular Young

Adult novel, *The Surprising Power of a Good Dumpling*, examines the deteriorating mental health of its protagonist Anna's mother. Reading it is powerful because it shows that people cannot simply be reduced to their mental illness — they are a mother, a wife, a friend — and also shows how such difficult, heartbreaking conditions manifest and affect family members. What I thought was really important about this novel was that it didn't necessarily tie up the mental illness thread in a neat bow. It's a real and meaningful depiction of chronic and severe mental illness, and the narrative depiction of it leaves a thought provoking and enduring impression that can meaningfully change perceptions.

So how does this happen?

As I've mentioned before, to completely answer that question, I'd need time and a thesis and a university library. However, in the interim, I'll give it a crack by putting forward the brief version of my hypothesis.

We need people to fit into a box in order to be able to feel safe around them; the 'box' of norms is a part of an evolutionary psychological set of ways that we as humans have developed in order to, very basically, not die. If someone behaves within a set of parameters that we've determined as 'normal', it's a shorthand way of allowing us to check off to ourselves that this person is very unlikely to kill us or take our stuff. When people don't fall into that box, we often treat them with social rejection because we don't feel that we can anticipate what they'll do, and thus we feel unsafe. That rejection can come in the simple form of edging away from them at a party, or as extreme as prejudicial violence.

In the instance of someone who falls into a minority because of immutable — or unchangeable — characteristics, be it sexuality, skin colour or neurodiversity, basically things which mean their behaviours seem to signal that they don't fit in the 'box' defined as 'normal', this overt 'difference' can be really dangerous for them depending on the circumstance and society in which they may be.

Stories help normalise and expand the definition of our normal 'box' to include the behaviours and norms of minority groups because they grant us access to the interior life of these groups. How exactly does that function? Well, remember Iser? Stories create a world where we suspend many of our pre-existing assumptions and biases and allow the story to take us where we will. As a result, we're more receptive to concepts and ideas that we may otherwise reject. In concert with the fact that we form a bond of sorts with the characters and story and thus cease to view someone within the story who's 'different', as such.

Put another way, the stories hold up a mirror to things we might not have seen before, or might have allowed our eyes to skip over, and they don't allow us to look anywhere else.

I don't want to be all dramatic and claim that one book has the power to change the world. That seems like a statement people would rush to disprove. I do think many books have the power to change the world, and one book has the power to touch a number of lives, to meaningfully invite reflection and consideration, and to be the first step to changing an attitude.

I'm not going to write about the responsibility of the author in crafting those narratives and in taking up a mantle of social change and cramming it into their works. I'm still trying to decide where I stand on that exact issue, but I definitely believe that readers and viewers generally know when they're being beaten over the head with a cause that's flimsily disguised as a book or film. I often worry that such an approach can push people away from a discussion.

When I write, I write about what's interesting to me, I write about the issues or ideas or themes I want to explore and deconstruct in greater depth. And I do that first and foremost for myself. I take what's familiar and examine it from a different angle, I invert it and run what is effectively a thought experiment in my head, which I then put down onto paper. I question what I see in the world around me, and that's the basis for my writing.

I don't want to speak for other writers or their processes. Although I'd be curious to know how they approach the inception of their stories.

I've been turning over and over in my mind the question of how we change the story.

How do we foster an acceptance, celebration,

and normalisation of LGBTQIA+ narratives, as an example? Holden Sheppard's 2019 novel, *Invisible Boys*, I'd argue, goes a long way toward providing one of the most nuanced portraits of the lived experience of young gay men in exploring just what so many people have to endure in order to be honest about who they are. On the flip side, the normalisation of same-sex relationships could arguably come through the totally accepted relationship of queer characters, such as in the *Girls of Paper and Fire* trilogy by Natasha Ngan (2018), or even as far back as David Levithan's *Boy Meets Boy* (2003), to pluck just two off the top of my head.

I suppose the only reticence that holds back my hand from penning a rallying cry is linked to something I said earlier — the assumption that all authors hold exactly the same views, and moreover, that those views are 'correct'.

Obviously, we can generally agree on the fact that discrimination on the basis of an immutable characteristic is wrong. But I think that the second you codify how best to go about that, the *instant* you define what that looks like, you actually limit your capacity to have a body of work that produces the most thoughtful, considered society.

In the long tradition of artists, I'll borrow from someone else, as I feel this particular sentiment better captures what I'm trying to say.

Neil Gaiman's 2012 'Make Good Art' commencement speech at Philadelphia's University of the Arts is a rallying cry to create, without telling people what to write. If you've not seen it, I recommend you take the time to watch (or read). Gaiman recommends telling the story that is unique to each of us, and to tell it in the *way* that is unique to each of us.

Write something true and that you enjoy writing. I think it's as simple as that. Those stories, the ones you write for yourself, and then ferociously refine so that they have the polish of a good piece of writing, I think those are the ones that reach people the best... and change them.

At the end of the day, your audience will make their own decisions, and come away with their own interpretations. People have pulled interpretations from my books that I certainly never intended to be there when I wrote them. The first thing I properly learned when I started studying poetry in school was that the piece's meaning is half what the author intended, and half what the reader takes away from it.

You can only control the words that go down on the page.

Make them good, make them true, and then hope that the people who pick up your work are transported into the world of the story, and even if they don't take away what you wanted them to, they are given *something* to consider.

At the end of the day, I think that's what a story is ultimately about: something that transports us, and along that journey, shows us something we might not have previously noticed. Without meaning to sound like a cliché, it's why my life is crafted around stories, because I believe they tell us intrinsic truths about the human condition, about who we are, and contain the paths to allow us to be better than we were.

It's magic in its purest form.

Works Cited

Books, Films, Plays

Birch, Tony. *The White Girl*. Brisbane: University of Queensland Press, 2019.

Brothers Grimm, The. *The Bicentennial Edition: The Annotated Brothers Grimm*. Tatar (trans.). New York: W.W. Norton & Company, 2012.

Butler, Judith. "Performative Acts and Gender Constitution." *Theatre Journal* 40.4 (1988): 519–531.

Chim, Wai. *The Surprising Power of a Good Dumpling*. Sydney: Allen & Unwin, 2019.

Cinderella. Dir. Clyde Geronimini, Wilfred Jackson, Hamilton Luske. Disney, 1950.

Cinderella. Dir. Kenneth Branagh. Disney, 2015.

Endacott, A B. *Dark Heart*. Independently Published, 2019.

Endacott, A B. *Dark Intent*. Independently Published, 2018.

Endacott, A B. *Dark Purpose*. Independently Published, 2019.

Endacott, A B. *King of the Seven Lakes*. Independently Published, 2018.

Endacott, A B. *Queendom of the Seven Lakes*. Independently Published, 2017.

Endacott, A B. *Ruthless Land*. Independently Published, 2018.

Gaiman, Neil. *Make Good Art*, William Morrow: New York, 2012.

Gaiman, Neil. *Sandman*. Graphic Novel series. Burbank: DC Comics, 1989–present.

Greene, Grahame. *The Quiet American*. Portsmouth: Heinemann, 1955.

Kauffman, Amie and Kristoff, Jay. *The Illuminae Files* series. New York: Knopf, 2015-2018.

Levithan, David. *Boy Meets Boy*. New York: Knopf, 2003.

Miyazaki, Hayao. *Princess Mononoke*. Tokyo: Studio Ghibli, 1997.

Morrison, Toni. *The Bluest Eye*. New York: Holt McDougal, 1970.

Ngan, Natasha. *Girls of Paper and Fire* trilogy. New York: Jimmy Patterson, 2017–present.

Nix, Garth. *The Old Kingdom* series. Sydney: Allen & Unwin, 1995–present.

Perrault, Charles. *Cendrillon*, 1697.

Shazam! Dir. David F. Samberg. Hollywood: Warner Bros, 2019.

Sheppard, Holden. *Invisible Boys*, Perth: Fremantle Press, 2019.

The Chilling Adventures of Sabrina. Dev. Roberto Aguirre-Sacasa. Netflix, 2018–present.

V for Vendetta. Dir. James McTeigue. Hollywood: Warner Bros, 2006.

Wright, Tom. *Black Diggers*. Playlab Theatre, premiered 2014.

Journal Articles, Academic Texts

Amerian, M., and Jofi, L. "Key Concepts and Basic Notes on Narratology and Narrative." *Scientific Journal of Review* 4.10 (2015): 182–192.

Barthes, R., and Duisit, L. "An Introduction to the Structural Analysis of Narrative." *New Literary History* 6.2 (1975): 237–272.

Byatt, A. S. "Introduction." *The Bicentennial Edition: The Annotated Brothers Grimm*, Tatar (trans.). New York: W.W. Norton & Company, 2004.

Chambliss, Julian C., Svitavsky, William L., and Fandino McFarland, Daniel (eds). *Assembling the Marvel Cinematic Universe: Essays on the Social, Cultural, and Geopolitical Domains*, Jefferson: McFarland & Company, 2018.

de Leeuw, Rebecca N. H., and van der Laan, Christa A. "Helping behavior in Disney Animated Movies and Children's Helping Behavior in the Netherlands." *Journal of Children and Media* 12.2 (2018): 159–174.

Dégh, L. "Grimm's "Household Tales" and Its Place in the Household: The Social Relevance of a Controversial Classic." *Western Folklore* 38.2 (1979): 83–10.

Geertz, Clifford. *The Interpretation of Cultures*. New York: Basic Books, 1973.

Iser, Wolfgang. *The Fictive and the Imaginary: Charting Literary Anthropology*. Baltimore: JHU Press, 1993.

Otto, Peter. "Romanticism, Modernity, and Virtual Reality: An Overview and Reconceptualisation of the Field." *Australian Humanities Review* 46, 2009.

Rojek, Chris. "Disney Culture." *Leisure Studies* 12.2 (1993): 121–135.

Ryan, Marie-Laure. "Narrative." *A Companion to Critical and Cultural Theory*. Eds. Sarah Blacker, Imre Szeman and Justin Sully. London: Blackwell, 2017. 517–30.

Tatar, Maria. "Preface: Magical and Mythical — Two Hundred Years of the Brothers Grimm." *The Bicentennial Edition: The Annotated Brothers Grimm*. Tatar (trans.), New York: W.W. Norton & Company, 2012.

Tatar, Maria. "Reading the Grimms' *Children's Stories and Household Tales*: Origins and Cultural Effects on the Collection." *The Bicentennial Edition: The Annotated Brothers Grimm*. Tatar (trans.), New York: W.W. Norton & Company, 2012.

Ward, Annelise R. *Mouse Morality: The Rhetoric of Disney Animated Film*. Austin: University of Texas Press, 2002.

Wasko, Janet. *Understanding Disney, The Manufacture of Fantasy*. Hoboken: Wiley, 2020.

Zipes, Jack. *The Original Folk and Fairy Tales of the Brothers Grimm. Foreign Rights Guide*. Princeton: Princeton University Press, 2014.

Online

Brandon, Emily. "Cinderella Writer Chris Weitz on the Magic it Took to Reinvent a Classic." *Oh.My.Disney* 16 Sept. 2015. Web. https://ohmy.disney.com/insider/2015/09/16/cinderella-writer-chris-weitz-on-the-magic-it-took-to-reinvent-a-classic/

Economist, The. "Disney Reigns Supreme Over the Film Industry." *The Economist* 2 Jan. 2020. Web. https://www.economist.com/graphic-detail/2020/01/02/disney-reigns-supreme-over-the-film-industry

Flood, Alison. "Brandon Sanderson: 'After a Dozen Rejected Novels, You Think Maybe This Isn't For You'."

The Guardian 23 Jul. 2020. Web. https://www.theguardian.com/books/2020/jul/23/brandon-sanderson-after-a-dozen-rejected-novels-you-think-maybe-this-isnt-for-you

"Kurt Vonnegut on the Shapes of Stories." *YouTube*. Uploaded by David Comberg, 30 October 2010.

Lussier, Germain, "Film Interview: Chris Weitz Talks Adapting Cinderella, Changing Directors, and Star Wars." *Slashfilm* 11 Mar. 2015. Web. https://www.slashfilm.com/chris-weitz-cinderella-interview/

McNary, Dave. "2018 Box Office Hits Record as Disney Dominates." *Variety* 2 Jan. 2020. Web. https://variety.com/2019/film/news/box-office-record-disney-dominates-1203098075/

"Queendom of the Seven Lakes by A B Endacott, Small Press Book Club." *YouTube*. Uploaded by Mad Cheshire Rabbit, 30 June 2020.

Rocha, Malu. "Why Do We Watch the Same Films and TV Shows Over and Over Again?" *Medium*. 23 Oct. 2019. Web. https://medium.com/@malu_rocha/why-do-we-watch-the-same-films-and-tv-shows-over-and-over-again-fbecfc67f3f0

Rosen, Christopher. "Hilary Duff Calls for Disney to Move *Lizzie McGuire* Reboot to Hulu." *Vanity Fair* 2 Mar. 2020. Web. https://www.vanityfair.com/hollywood/2020/02/lizzie-mcguire-disney-reboot-drama

Variety. "Love Simon Spinoff Series Moves from Disney Pluss to Hulu." *NBC News* 26 February 2020. Web. https://www.nbcnews.com/feature/nbc-out/love-simon-spinoff-series-moves-disney-plus-hulu-n1142636

Viswanath, Jake. "Hilary Duff Remains Optimistic About the Lizzie McGuire Reboot." *Bustle* 23 July 2020. Web.

https://www.bustle.com/entertainment/hilary-duffs-lizzie-mcguire-reboot-update

Yorke, John. "All Stories Are the Same." *The Atlantic* 1 Jan. 2016. Web. https://www.theatlantic.com/entertainment/archive/2016/01/into-the-woods-excerpt/421566/

Acknowledgements

Somewhat contrary to my expectations, writing a piece of semi-academic non-fiction requires that far more people be thanked than at the end of publishing a full-length novel. It's true to say that in academia, you stand upon the shoulders of the thinkers who have come before you, and indeed, you are boosted there by people who are older, and far cleverer than you. My thanks, to that end, first and foremost to Dr David McInnis, Professor Peter Otto, and Dr Joe Hughes of the University of Melbourne School of Culture and Communication, as well as Associate Professor Sarah Wills of the University of Melbourne Faculty of Arts. This piece began life as a journal article, heavily influenced by a PhD proposal. My application was unsuccessful, but the time, generosity, and intelligence that I was fortunate enough to receive was truly staggering. Thank you so much for your support and encouragement, and for your assistance in crafting that proposal.

I have already dedicated this Mini to her, but thanks must then come to Katherine Larsen, founder and director of Debut Books. Her support as a reader of my fiction work, and the fact that she found a purpose for a proposal and article I loved but wasn't quite sure where exactly they belonged, inspires enormous gratitude in me. Kat, your vision for Debut Books is amazing, and I have no doubt that it will realise every bit of its potential. Thank you so much for trusting me to be the first thing you publish.

Next thanks goes to Amy Lovat—behind every great book is a great editor. Your insight improved this immeasurably. And thank you to Jason Nahrung, who edits my fiction work. If the job was even a little bit easy for Amy, it was because working with you has made me a better writer.

Of course, the point at which anything appears

in print is only the tip of the iceberg. My usual thanks to my amazing family, incredible friends, and wonderful partner stand in perpetuity.

Finally, thank you to the books that have changed me and the people who wrote them. They are far too multitudinous to list, but without those words, I simply would not be who I am today.

And, if you'll allow me one postscript. Thank you, dear reader, for picking up this collection of my thoughts, and sticking with it through to the end. I hope that at the very least, it's given you some food for thought. Ultimately, that's all any book can really do.

Alice Boér-Endacott
December 2020

Alice Boér-Endacott is a Melbourne-based author whose published works include six fantasy titles.

With an academic background in Anthropology, French, Executive Management, and Islamic Politics (four fields that aren't necessarily considered natural combinations), and nearly a decade of work in and around high schools teaching and tutoring English, Creative Writing, and Debating (three areas that *are* often considered reasonably natural combinations), she finds writing the way to combine and express the myriad of thoughts and ideas circling around her head.

When she isn't writing, she's either thinking about writing, or eating, and very occasionally performing the role of Secretary for LoveOzYA (an organisation that seeks to champion Australian Young Adult literature).

She is a cat person, travel lover, and adorer of chocolate and wine.

You can find out more by visiting her website, abendacott.com, or following her on Instagram (@alicejaneboere), or Twitter (@ajendacott).